My Spanglish Es Impecable

My Spanglish Es Impecable

Poems by

Lynn Ciesielski

© 2026 Lynn Ciesielski. All rights reserved.
This material may not be reproduced in any form, published,
reprinted, recorded, performed, broadcast,
rewritten or redistributed without
the explicit permission of Lynn Ciesielski.
All such actions are strictly prohibited by law.

Cover design by Shay Culligan
Cover image by Mike Bacos on Unsplash
Author photo by Mike Niman, 2025

ISBN: 978-1-63980-841-0
Library of Congress Control Number: 2026931927

Kelsay Books
502 South 1040 East, A-119
American Fork, Utah 84003
Kelsaybooks.com

For my Spanish teacher, Miriam, with whom I've studied via social media for nearly eight years, and finally met in person last summer. Miriam is remarkable, kind, and vibrant, and she motivates me to learn even when the work is challenging. The time I spent with her and her family in Guatemala inspired a number of the poems in this book.

¡Gracias por todo, Miriam! Muchos abrazos. ¡Te amo!

Acknowledgments

Thank you to the following publications, in which versions of these poems previously appeared:

Buffalo News: "Waiting for Huevos"

Weekly Avocet: "Alone in the Andes"

Tilting Toward the Moon: LitGarden Writers Anthology II (LitGarden Writers, 2023): "Alone in the Andes"

Contents

Author's Note	11
First Words	17
What I Learned From My Spanish Teacher	19
We Took the Chicken Bus	22
At the Water Hole	24
How to Cure Montezuma's Revenge	27
In Little Havana	30
Confession	33
Andes Horizon	34
Menagerie	36
Where the Whole City Is Rated R	38
Settled	40
Waiting for Huevos	42
Diversion	44
While the Others Sleep	46
Lost in San Andrés	47
Seen From the Balcony	49
Reverie	50
Bucket List	52
Barriers	54
Musing About Passion Fruit	56
Underground	58
Grandfather's Wine	60
Un Poco Loco	62
Alone in the Andes	64

Author's Note

I first became intrigued by South and Central America when I was in high school. The study of the ancient Maya and Incan cultures fascinated me and I romanticized these indigenous peoples to an extent. The concept of colonialism appalled me, and I resented the Spaniards for their attempted annihilation of entire languages, religions, and cultures. For whatever reason, I did not study Spanish in school, favoring French for what I then considered its superior beauty. After four years in high school and a semester in college, I barely speak a word of French.

My Spanglish, however, is impeccable.

In my early thirties, I traveled to Cancun and Isla Mujeres, Mexico. Prior to the trip, I looked up a short list of travel words and phrases that might help me. That was my first real exposure to Spanish.

My false confidence got me in a bit of trouble as you'll read in my poem, "First Words". Still, I had a wonderful time, saw incredible Mayan ruins at Chichen Itza, enjoyed the unmatchable experience of attending the quinceañera of a Mexican teen who my companion, Bonita, befriended, and I took my first snorkeling trip in the Caribbean where I encountered amazing sea creatures like octopus, starfish, and clown fish up close.

The stomach problems I experienced were not so wonderful, as I illustrate in "How to Cure Montezuma's Revenge".

Back home I still had a preschooler to care for and a teaching career, so not much time for travel. My interest had been sparked, though.

I took every opportunity to pick up Spanish here and there, listening to Puerto Ricans in my city of Buffalo and grabbing as many words as I could.

It was almost two decades before I returned to Latin America. Thrilled to learn that a poet friend, Sara, and her partner, Tad, were teaching English in Colombia, I decided to visit them in the colonial pueblo of Villa de Leyva. My husband at the time was concerned about my difficulty with the language so he suggested a Puerto Rican friend of his accompany me.

For the first couple days we stayed in Bogotá in a trendy hostel in the barrio of Candelaria, populated largely by students and bohemians. There I met Gabriella, named after the poet/teacher/freedom fighter, Gabriella Mistral, huge heroine in Latin America. Young Gabriella worked at the hostel as a concierge while she attended school for journalism.

We spoke every morning, she tolerating my spotty Spanish though her English was flawless and it would have been easier for both of us to speak in my native tongue. When I left, we exchanged addresses and became pen pals for a time so I could practice Spanish.

Villa de Leyva was phenomenal. Walking on cobblestones reminded me daily that I wasn't thirty anymore and I really could stand to get in shape. Yet sunrise over the Andes was como nada más, the people welcomed you like family, and the fruits were phenomenal, fresh, and inexpensive. I had a wonderful visit with my friends and left eager to learn more Spanish. Sara worked with me for a time, doing lessons on social media.

Several years later, I returned to Colombia, this time alone. It was daring, but I tend to be a thrill seeker. I made plans to stay in the hostel I remembered in Candelaria.

Gabriella no longer worked there, but she was interested in meeting up. She rode three buses from her pueblo far from Bogotá. We hiked in a wooded park and had lunch at a well-known spot where they serve traditional food. I ate my favorite, ajiaco, a uniquely flavored chicken soup with potatoes and corn and Gabriella ordered a tamale. There was so much food, neither of us could finish.

After two days in Bogotá, I took the long bus ride down to Villa de Leyva, the place I had so adored. Ana Maria, Sara's favorite young student who I'd met on my first trip, played tour guide for four days. After hiking again in the Andes' foothills with Ana Maria, watching the opening ceremonies of the Olympics with her mother and her aged aunt, and having a three-course lunch in a relaxed cafe, I got the bus back to Bogotá.

The next morning, I boarded a plane to the tropical island of San Andrés, the southernmost island in the Caribbean, variously owned by Colombia and Nicaragua. Sara and Tad were teaching there at that point.

I stayed with Marlyn, a Raizal woman with a huge personality and an even bigger heart. I snorkeled every day, and because Marlyn insisted I speak Spanish in her home, my language continued to improve.

Soon after I returned from this journey to Colombia, I met my Spanish Teacher, Miriam Hernandez. We worked in a group on

Skype with three other students who were advanced far beyond me. I struggled to catch up and learned quite a bit along the way but still felt lost. About two years into my study, very overwhelmed and frustrated as the already advanced students continued to advance, I dropped out of the class.

Another two years later, I started kicking myself for spending so much time studying a foreign language, making fair progress, only to quit midstream. I contacted Miriam and she agreed to take me on as a solo student. I progressed much more easily as I worked at my own rate and even better, I developed a terrific friendship with Miriam.

I made one more trip to Colombia, this time with an acquaintance and her daughter Karen. There were some adventures and some trials, but they ended up falling in love with Colombia just as I had.

Last year I finally had the opportunity to visit my teacher, Miriam, in Guatemala. She welcomed me into her home just as she has and continues to do with many of her students.

The trip was amazing, and I experienced so much love among her immediate and extended family and neighbors. We had terrific adventures, and she nursed me when I was sick.

My knowledge of Spanish has become very valuable as I work as a volunteer in a food pantry that serves a fair number of Latin Americans. Another result of my travels and my Spanish study has been that I was able produce this book.

I hope my poetry will spark your interest in Latin American culture and in Spanish.

¡Muchas gracias por leerlo!

—Lynn Ciesielski

First Words

The Cancun beach bar sings siren songs
of salsa and surf and I can't resist.
Leading with a smile, I strut in, wearing
a bikini top, tropical wrap 'round my hips and
appropriated cornrows in my stringy-gringa-hair,
determined to show off all thirty Spanish phrases
I memorized on the plane:

¿Cómo te llamas? What is your name?
¿Podrías invitarme una cerveza? Could you buy me a beer?
¿Dónde está el baño? Where is the bathroom?
¿Eres estudiante? Are you a student?
¿Podrías tomarte una foto conmigo? Could you take a photo with me?

Muscle-shirted hombres lean close, their machismo
smelling of Tommy Bahama cologne.
They talk to me in habanero-hot, liquid voices,
breaking waves of Spanish punctuated with snickers.

No comprendo, I say. *Sola hablo un poco.*
I only speak a little.

Claro tu sabes. Nosotros queremos lo mismo.
Of course you know. We want the same thing.

Expletives fly but I pick out *gringa* and *puta,* words
learned from Puerto Rican classmates years ago.

In the States there were codes women used to alert
bartenders that a cab is needed pronto, but

at this beach bar, there weren't even roads.

I excuse myself to el baño, bury myself among tourists
and slip out the back, panting, wishing I'd limited
my Spanish to, *No hablo español.*

What I Learned From My Spanish Teacher

1.

The surest way to remember how to conjugate
pluscuamperfecto tense is to write 40 sentences
for homework instead of 10 by mistake.

2.

In a place like San Pedro, family, community,
and church mean more than money, a car,
or a fancy house—people who wonder why
she's never ridden an airplane don't realize
there's no reason to leave.

3.

Chicken buses don't always carry chickens
and the best way to handle getting pecked at is to
avoid showing your feathers.

4.

If I ask enough questions during the conversation
section, I can occasionally avoid being forced
to conjugate an irregular verb in 14 tenses,
but *solo ocasionalmente.*

5.

One of the things that makes our relationship unique
is that we are exactly—down to the day—10 years apart.

6.

She's just as willing to learn as to teach, and the hour
I spend giving her yoga instruction while her husband
Henry watches amused is priceless.

7.

Certain volcanoes spout steam, not smoke, and she can prove it by showing me the view from her back window.

8.

I work harder and learn faster if she doesn't let on that she speaks English until I advance to the more difficult work.

9.

There are six love languages, not five, and the sixth one is teaching.

We Took the Chicken Bus

Four a.m., quick coffee, no breakfast.
We'll stop for gas and pastry on the way.
Miriam, Henry, Daena and I walk to the square,
await the chicken bus.

My Spanish teacher spoke of these rickety
Guatemalan buses that stop for farmers
to board with chickens for auction.
Off we ride to a place familiar as a water park,
though pueblos and volcanoes make it brand new.

In pairs and threes, riders arrive, hugs all around,
cousins, in-laws, uncles, aunts, nephews, nieces,
so much family, and all neighbors.

For five hours we sit cramped, stop for breakfast, gas,
but no chickens.

I joke with Henry,

Where are the chickens? Your wife promised chickens.

He says, *You're the chicken. Pollo blanca.*

I peck back with a laugh, *Pollo marrón.*

We arrive at the park, buy tickets, rent lockers,
remove shoes, then squeeze knee to knee
into *Catapault*'s huge tube. Drop. Land—Splash!
Swirl crazy 'round *Tornado* on rubber mats.
Slam sides, twist, spill—a few bruises—Ouch!

A sign appeals to Miriam: *Lazy River—
A relaxing float along a winding waterway.*

Boring . . . but I comply—a short break may be okay
after those wild rides, but that doesn't last.
Relax is what I do in my sleep.
Lazy River becomes *Bumper Inner Tubes*.
We slam, slosh, splash 'round bends, gushing waves,
relaxing as a roller coaster.

At the end of the ride, Miriam finds her glasses gone.
¡*Mis gafas! ¡Las necesito! My glasses! I need them!*

Daena and I check the Lost and Found. The glasses—
twisted, mangled, bent.

At the Water Hole

The guidebook says:
The Guatemalan jungle is best enjoyed
when you embark before dawn,
listen to life even before you see it.

But circumstance makes its own rules.

Daena and I had drank Gallos at the pool bar,
'til long after midnight when they threw us out.
We slept until nine, split at ten.

On the bus, children stretch through frames
where windows might have been,
far as arms will reach.
Parents clasp their narrow hips to keep
the rest of their bodies inside.
Along the road, signs warn *Jaguar Crossing*
in pictures, and in Spanish, *Keep Hands Inside.*
The tourists, oblivious, with a taste for excitement,
wish a panther would come close enough to pose,
so they can brag back home how they almost became dinner.

The driver arrives at the Tikal Park entrance.
We disembark; no jaguar, puma, panther.
What approaches is a coati, the raccoon's relative,
with its pesky manner.
Nuisance critter, as the guide describes.

The tourists feed them so they hang around.
People have been bitten, but they don't learn.

I long to spot a spider monkey, so I ask our guide
to point one out,
Por favor, muestrame un mono.

The guide has a line-up, lots to see at Tikal,
Temple of the Great Jaguar, Temple of the Mask, the canals.
We climb, view vistas, photograph canopies, carvings.
Daena bubbles with joy—her Art History class in real time.

At the top of the tallest temple, the sky electrifies.
As quick as we can, we flee to lower ground,
but before we reach, the rainforest justifies its name.
Delicious! I say—rain in the jungle—torrents.
I thank the sky for doing just what it should.
Drops hopscotch from my poncho, puddle below.
Minutes later, the sun rages again, inhales the water
while the ground sucks in the rest.

At last, we walk in search of fauna.
The guide points to a tree, *Tucán!*
Daena cheers though I miss it,
then thinking the tour will end soon, I whine,
Pero los monos! But the monkeys!

The guide chuckles, touches forearm to lips,
somehow makes a sound like a file
rubbed against the skin of a wet balloon.
We wander from tree to towering Ceiba tree
as he repeats his call.

I miss a step as the guide cries out, *¡Mira! ¡Monos!*
High above, in a clearing among the canopy,
spider monkeys!
A mom swings from branch to branch,
baby on her back.
She plucks fruit, feeds him, swings again.
Her long, strong arms and fingertips laugh at gravity.

The party starts. We wander tree to tree,
Daena videotapes the action, and the monkeys,
so reclusive an hour ago, perform at every turn.
Monkeys in the jungle!

¡Qué emocionante!

How to Cure Montezuma's Revenge

The first time food brings me to my knees,
my vacation in Cancun.
Grilled chorizo from a street vendor
on the plaza—greasy, savory, sinful meat.
Flavored with mayo, baked all day in tropical sun.

The rest of the day, my stomach throws tantrums.
All night on the bathroom floor, my head
swirls visions of the Mayan suicide goddess.

When I awaken, my plane ticket home is *gone*.
I panic, then telephone my travel agent
who steers me to a local branch.
I hand a cab driver the address,
no idea where I'm going, or whether I'll arrive.
Curled like a snail in the back seat, I pray.
Somehow I return to the plaza, ticket in hand.

There, fruit stands, cafés, captivating aromas
greet my returning appetite, but logic tells me
packaged lunch meats from the supermarket,
the kind I avoid at home, have enough chemicals
to kill the bacteria that might make me sick.
I eat baloney and processed cheese the rest of my trip.

Next venture in Guatemala, it's the beans—
breakfast beans with huevos, jugo and pan,
lunchtime beans with sopa, queso, and flan,

dinner beans with papas, maíz and jamón.
I think I'll be safe with beans, but by day two,
my only jaunts are from toilet to bed.

Third day, I dare a ride to Antigua, five-star lunch:
chicken in cream sauce, spinach, pasta—no beans.
Still my stomach twists and heaves,
a rugged walk back to the bus, cobblestone streets.
I duck into a shop on the way, heave into the privy.

By evening, my stomach stills, but next morning,
I pass on beans, ease through breakfast bread.
Miriam plans a picnic lunch in her nearby garden.
We walk the three miles to the supermercado,
buy sandwich stuff, fruit, soft drinks.
Still weak, but to be a proper guest,
I walk with my crew to the garden venue.
After four grapes, I sit out the picnic
in a bathroom that sandwiches me like a pupusa.

Back at the house, Miriam picks orégano fresco,
brews a tea that tastes like the weed tea
the local bully made me drink when I was a kid.

Still, it helps, so for the rest of the trip, I drink
only *la medicina natural* and satisfy my hunger
with sweet conversations and rich sunsets.

In Little Havana

It's another world here, where vintage cars
in mint condition cruise by, just like in Cuba.
At the 50s style diner, we trade
steamy Miami breezes for hot tango music
on the transistor radio, café fuerte
steeped in a cafetera, served with
Carnation Milk by waitresses whose
cleavage is deep as the Caribbean and
undulates like the surf.

The menu is carefully chalked on a board
in impeccable Spanglish, so more customers
can order traditional choices like
Cuban Sandwiches, pastelillos, and bistec.
I choose what I came for, the famous Cuban.
My husband (at least for now) requests a steak.
I excuse myself and take the long, winding walk
to el baño, but once there, I change my mind.
In the sink, I find a giant cucaracha belly up.
I hold my breath not to inhale something foul
and walk-run the maze back to the table
to find my food waiting for me.

I'm not hungry, I say, *You're not gonna believe . . .*
then, *Who is she?* nodding toward a woman
who walks away with a briefcase, winking at Nick.

Nick says, *Ohh, hon . . . have I got a story for you! We're all minding our business and she walks in. She sets down her case, opens it and gets to business. One by one she pulls out a camisole, see-through brassiere, tong . . .*

You mean thong, I say . . .

Yeah, yeah, whatever, Nick answers, then continues,

But it doesn't end there.
She slips behind the chalkboard again and again
then models each item while the men moan
and the women groan.
All at once, the manager comes out, hollering,
threats to have her arrested.

She apologizes with a sloppy kiss.
The manager blushes and orders her to get dressed.

My eyes widen, wondering whether this is another one of Nick's lies, or an example of truth being stranger than fiction.

I say, *Maybe we should just leave.*

Nick responds, *But your food is here. Mine is so delicious. I wanted you to buy yourself something. I'll get her back here. You can tell me your story while you pay the check.*

Confession

The wailing infant's mom shoves a plug
in his mouth, and his screams finally subside.
I make out a few familiar phrases in the streams
of Spanish chatter that slip into the pockets
of silence, listening like a mediocre linguist.

I sink into the clouds that surround our plane,
lulled by the whirring motor,
the muffled conversation and the bustle
of the flight attendant passing through
with bilingual offers of coffee,
soda, and biscotti como nada más.

Nearing our destination, we survey Bogotá:
the Andes, smog, congested streets,
as the child's cries crescendo anew.
The blood rushes through my brain,
nearly into my sinuses.

I feel no remorse when the impulse hits to
smash a window and hurl the baby, flailing
to his death, heedless of the risks
an open window would pose to us all.

I burrow my hands beneath my thighs,
drive my feet into the floor,
and wince at the metal taste of the blood
my teeth draws from my lower lip

as I struggle to resist wailing myself.

Andes Horizon

Skyline settles in my soul.
Terra-cotta houses hide in the fog
among craggy peaks.
I crave the rich tones of Colombian coffee,
even the air thick with its aroma.

Too early, the locals sound asleep in their beds.
So I skip the coffee; the leaves I chew
keep the buzz running, a fair substitute
if I take enough to sustain the heavy climb,
up both ways, like the old dad jokes go.

Soon the sky heralds daybreak, spilling
vivid purple, rich rose, luminous yellow.
Carlos Vives sings in my head:

Parte del aire de los recuerdos
de aquellos besos que se fueron en invierno.
Part the air of the memories
of those kisses made in winter.

But our kisses feel much further away
than a continent and three seasons
and I'll never *sleep in your hair* again.

Vives' songs remind me why I travelled
so far alone with no return ticket.

The rain gushes, rinsing the songs from my head.
Roosters replace music, joined with sounds
of shutters, doors and calls of *Buen día*
from nearby café owners.
Coffee will soon clear my foggy thoughts, but the fog
settled among Andes peaks will forever continue
to harbor the magic of my singular
Colombian dream.

Menagerie

In Bogotá, steep streets rise with steps,
then spill down with ramps. Aqueducts stream
after daily rain, a maze of traps to slip me up.

Push carts display coca leaves and THC tincture,
teasing out memories of my youthful sprees.
I ask the young vendor how much tincture it takes.

Two grams, she says.

Giggling, I tell the story of the night I chewed
fifteen grams of edibles just to help me sleep.
The floor rolled. My brain whirled. Dreams married fog,
honeymooning among condors.
Her eyes darken like the sky above as she protests,

No mami. No. ¡Peligrosa! Dangerous. ¡Qué loco!

My llama gaze transfixes her wisdom,
yet I nod and walk away.

All around crowds teem—vendors peddle
fruit cups, handicrafts, rum shots, sweet, lukewarm tea
spiked with aguardiente.

We share obleas—wafers sandwiched with dulce de leche,
chopped nuts, blackberry puree.

Plastic cups hold melon, mango, pineapple,
so luscious my mouth salsas.

Where the Whole City Is Rated R

Bogotá lovers don't mind
if their tangled limbs and lips
crowd narrow sidewalks, ousting
singles into screeching traffic.

Everyone knows that three is a crowd.

I exhale the steam from several blocks
of couples into the cool evening air,
then duck into my escape,
Café Para Dos, although I am just one.
There I order that luscious passion fruit dessert.

Savoring each taste, I pull out my notes
to conjugate, *amo, amas, amán.*

They love? I ask, glancing at the couple
stretched on the settee, encircled by rose petals
and backed by a nude mural.
He feeds her strawberries and lines,

Mi amor, nunca ha habido otra.
There has never been another,

with a hand drifting up her skirt.

The music is more a throbbing prompt
than a melody in this dimly lit
telenovela scene.
Where I'm from, no doubt, someone would say,

Get a room.

Here the whole city doubles as boudoir.

Settled

Sometimes I can only whisper sand.
Words wither in Spanish as in English,
though stories beg so many lines.
My schooling fails as I back-step
to count the age of bones pressed in bedrock
on cobbles that remind me of my own aging bones,
yet support my awkward tread, so that

even as I stumble, I sink into
this Andes cradle so warm somehow
despite its hard, cold terrain.

La gente, siempre fuerte, rise up to reach
beyond genocide, division, granite ground
that will not sprout for years, despite their travails.
They search the sky from where their god surveys,
then surmise,

It is dry because we are selfish.

Yet I meet doñas, total strangers, who when I ask them
to point out the path, lead me to cafés,
share hot drinks, rich and dark,
and the larger share of their galletas
or pastelillos with guava paste.

Waiting for Huevos

In the mountain's morning chill,
at a polished hardwood table
just round enough for notebook, pen,
and inches of bare from arc to center,
I shrink myself, gaze dropping,
then telescoping forward.

Dead-end, an aged doña glides
back and forth from a boxy kitchen
toward my space where she
invites herself into my morning
with a smile and *¿Cómo está?*

I order in mosaic Spanish, hoping
her arepa is better than the brown-black,
crumbly corn paste I got
from yesterday's Bogotá vendor.

When, in seconds, the señora returns,
I re-arrange my oaken disc
for jugo fresco and café fuerte, shrinking
to a foreign world far larger than the self I bring,
where a hat tree is stacked with gaucho brims,
felt, rattan, and alpaca,
phallic cactus in a clay Muisca head,
and adobe walls sturdy over centuries,
yet a whisper to the Andes peaks.

The eggs, when they come, share the table
con la mejor arepa con queso,
and the thick forearm of Jose Antonio,
the hotel owner, whose chatter reminds me
that in Villa de Leyva nothing is mine alone,
not table, nor sunrise, nor silence.

Although he'd offer todos los huevos,
arepas and café to any paying customer,

the true gifts of life could not be owned.

And even a pad-locked room in Colombia
couldn't bar entry to a scorpion.

Diversion

My *sonrisa* widens to a daybreak
on this near-equator Andes peak,
where only a fool would question why
the Spanish smile and English sunrise
are almost the same word.

So, determined to write verse
beneath this honey-laden sky,
where a mug of family-farmed coffee
from last night's café was poetry already,

I stumble down curving, cobblestone roads
with no signs nor divisions,
where vehicles, stray dogs, and pedestrians
move as one, horns honk at random,
and, if time to time a truck flattens me
to a store-front, I deflate for safety,
then step out again with other foot travelers.

Realizing I'm no further along, I ask a local,

¿Dónde está la plaza?

Her answer is a confounding question,

¿La plaza del mercado o la plaza principal?

And I know I don't need the market,
though Sara's delicious descriptions
and las doñas with macaw-striped baskets,
red woven skirts and thread-laced blouses
wiggle my will to write, even while knowing

this moment may never return, so pretending
to understand, I smile, say, *Gracias*, and walk,
until the tumble of cobbles, cultures and words
spills me to a place where finding
what I want means less than wanting what I find.

I follow the doñas, the colors, the Saturday
morning tradition, allowing el mercado
to choose me.

While the Others Sleep

I string the stars point to point, connecting
these lights that sparkle overhead tonight,
then gaze toward town, where Christmas lights hang,
and feel a magic, so profound and great.

The twisted rail winds 'round the amazing
ceramic stairs in terra cotta red.
Glazed and brilliant mosaics emblazon
this four-story climb to my Andean bed.

Your glinting eyes appear, complementing
the cosmic masterpiece and I am home.
As my papasan swings, Shakira sings
into my headset, inspiring a poem.

From the yard, the roosters croon their own song,
their voices crying out a dozen strong.

Lost in San Andrés

The salt from our skin mixes with sea air
as we spill down streets where shops
flaunt cheap imports, sarongs, and local rum.
At every corner, we meet beachfront.

Mapless, we fumble, seeking dinner and supplies,
immersed in a mangled maze, until something
murmurs a memory: Marlyn carting me
the few miles to market on her moto.

So, following the trail eroded by six rainy seasons,
I lead Karen and her mom through tropic air,
across streets where horns and screeches
replace stop signs and signals.

Six turns and an hour later, Karen bleats, *A market!*
We stock up: factory-farmed coffee, creamer,
and a plastic bag of water with a spout,
all in a cloth carry sack.

As we leave the market, the sky heaves, but the tide
in our bellies rises, and Karen insists on U.S. chain food.
Relying on GPS navigation distorted by the island's
horseshoe shape, we spend an hour chasing her cravings.

She settles for Colombian-style shawarma,
with beverages in paper sacks. Then we seek
the Airbnb we abandoned on an unnamed beach.
The sky makes mayhem like it only can in the tropics

and our dinner bag starts to melt. Karen's tears join
the storm, flooding the food further
and she shelters, fussing with her dead phone.
With no GPS, she finally concedes to hail a cab.
We spot an empty livery; I ask someone where the driver is.

When he appears, Karen powers up my working phone
and shows him a screenshot of our lodging.
He joins the chaos, skidding down stormy streets,
up one block, around a corner, down another block
We arrive at our misplaced Airbnb, just two blocks away.

Seen From the Balcony

It was an outcry, a rebellion built of repression,
against Christian colleges where youth danced
six inches apart and skirt lengths were measured
by stretching fingertips down toward hems.

That year's spring break throbbed with salsa,
shouts, and stomps. Revelers on deck threw final papers
overboard, then dove in after them, and sorority sisters
danced in time with their swimming strokes.

At eleven p.m., curfew loomed, so they downed
their final rum drinks, feeling the undertow that fought
the frolic and won, dragging them deeper into a sea
where chaos is more predictable than smooth sailing,

and only seafarers ride the swell, while common partiers
kiss the rocks. Smashed, as they were,
they didn't feel much but drowned in the drink.

From my balcony perch, I watched, crying, *¡Baila! Dance!*

But they sank and spilled in the surf and the Jesuits cried out,
Holy Mother, pray for them.

Reverie

At a fair distance, the party boat throbs
with shouts and stomps from revelers
who save all year to trade the pound
of workaday Bogotá streets for the slap
of the surf and the burn of the rum.

Its lights replace the constellations clouds mask
with engineered glimmer, electrifying the night.

From my sixth-story perch, fireworks alert me
that it is midnight and I am still awake.

All at once, an undertow tugs my feet, pulling me
seaward and I submit, bare beneath my nightshirt.

Sand slithers up through my toes, drawing me in;
the brine rinses the sticky air from my flesh.

I lie supine, buoyant, bobbing in the blue,
unaware that the sea has captured me.
When I stretch my feet to reach the seabed,
there is no bottom to be found.

Bucket List

In the *sea of seven colors,* the inboard boat
reels us into the depths, where
gorgeous coral and tiger sharks live.

Reggaetón rocks our bodies while rum
rocks our souls and steels our nerves.
Soon we'll be airborne, aloft beneath
a smiling orange chute.

Tranquila, the captain's mate assures,
setting the first pair loose.

With these chutes, you are buoyant as
the cormorants you'll transcend.

Reeling, we swallow our fear with another
shot of Plantation rum,
and the mate readies us for flight.
After handing us jackets and helping us
climb into harnesses, he hooks our D-rings
to the chute we'll share on our tandem ride.

In moments, we scoot our bottoms to the edge
of the deck, until the motor's speed
and the wind's thrust lift us and we glide,
thirty stories high and more.

Succumbing to my body's resistance to stay upright,
I lean back, head hanging, hands high,
and marvel at the San Andrés skyline behind us.

Pastel edifices, oval coast and prolific mangroves
blow kisses that dissipate in the wind.

We glide—dip—
rise—higher—up—down—

At last we splash hard, feet and legs smacking
the cool Caribbean, then up—another ten meters
down—suave—slide seated—
upon the deck, greeted with whoops, hollers, sighs.

Barriers

for Terez

1.

When they speak the language not theirs,
do full worlds fall off, or does
their immutable lyric bridge that chasm
where words and culture unclasp?
Do fingertips touch 'cross oceans, transcend
that lost link, or does the void itself
become the shared entity, that vehicle to carry them
from oblivion into existence?
And how does it ever begin in the beginning?

2.

She, me, we met via poetry,
emotion, her words then
years of glimpses, Facebook posts, no more,
when upon return from Colombia, craving
a new idioma, scrolling posts, I came upon hers,
from Spain, the mother land? Show me?
En español, claro, and so it went,
messages, quick notes, conversations,
my Spanish spotty, hers an adopted child.
Yet they flowered, my language, our friendship
through winter, spring, her home then just
several states away until November, a year since
germ stage, she wrote me,

This teaching stint, love it and all, nice place
but so uncertain, those grants, you know?
You never know.
Time to head back.

Spain? Colombia? Not Latvia?

Buffalo. Yes. Buffalo.
We'll do coffee.

3.

Our reunion, mutual meeting, shared hugs,
then who, what, in this landscape of English,
are we? Strangers once more.
To begin from the beginning or where?
Spanish? Yes! Where we knew each other best,
Then later with English-only speakers, I wonder,

Who is this woman of Facebook posts,
handy Spanish guides, time lapse replies?

And we together sit, shared table, separate capsules,
stretching to shrink the distance.

Musing About Passion Fruit

Passion melts me beneath the late August sun,
on a two-hour stroll through blooming Buffalo
barrios, and desire strikes, *ice cream,*
passion fruit or maracuyá as I first learned it.
Maritza's poem about her initial taste had
taunted me, painting a sultry scene,
clandestine romance, Colombian beach,
urging my first sampling.
She had messaged me the prior day
from that Bogotá café where I first enjoyed it.

You've succeeded, a perfect recreation,
The café, the decadent dessert. ¡Perfecto!

I continue on my walk, rekindling my love
for this charmed locale I call home,
no mountains nor sea, just passion, maracuyá
ice cream whispering from my freezer.

My friend Michael texts, *Hmmm. Ice cream?*
Flowering cityscapes? Yes!
But a rain check for another sunny day.

A ring and it's Carm, a poet who knows
Maritza and passion, rosy like maracuyá,
so still craving, I invite her to share
that incredible flavor with me.

Two miles remaining on my path, my feet freeze
and my resolve melts, so I choose to wait
for the metro, the woman next to me
scatting jazz tunes, with steamy passion on this
heated maracuyá day.

Underground

We pay the fee, sign the waiver; it's official.
Bona fide spelunkers, we wear simple helmets
equipped with lamps, three levels of light,
Daena sports flip-flops, me sturdy sneakers,
with the resolve of women ready for adventure.

The initial twenty-step descent barely prepares me
for the challenging navigations that await.
We soon find ourselves on slippery, broken
limestone slopes and Daena steadies me
as I'm less assured than she's ever seen.

In fast-Spanish, the guide describes formations,
stalactites, stalagmites, all with clever names.
I catch twenty percent, focused on my footing.
Daena suggests I aim for the deepest wells;
I soak my sneakers in muddy lime-water.

We dip, duck, panic at the sight of a drop low enough
to challenge a skilled limbo dancer,
then realize it leads in the wrong direction, so turn around.
We pick up the pace, familiar with the landscape,
with a sigh of relief that we'd chosen the shorter route.

Baby bats are the best part, huddled in crevices,
but the darkness obscures photo-documentation.
A giant spider with wiry legs and bulbous body
and two centipedes flesh out the sparse wildlife.
Cockroaches, they say, would survive a nuclear attack.

Grandfather's Wine

Behind the window a row of bottles
labeled simply, *El Vino del Abuelo,*
The Wine of the Grandfather.

Miriam motions us through an alley
to an enclave, paved with rough granite,
sprouting with weeds beneath our feet.

Surrounding us, trellises; above, grapevines
with a single bunch of concords, so purple
and ready to burst, I reach for one.

A cheerful *¡Bienvenidos!* interrupts me,
and a weary-eyed, wizened abuelo
ushers me toward his offerings.

Our bench fronts a table, scattered with bottles
I mistake for vinegar at first.
with twist tops and an ancient layer of dust.

Abuelo offers us flavors I had never linked with wine:
coffee, basil, strawberry, then pours sips into flimsy cups
like those used for pills in hospitals.

I struggle not to spill these cups that buck
every attempt to drink.
A warm tingle spreads, flavors masking each other

until instinct signals me to cleanse my palate.
I request water, swish, spit, taste a few more.
Eight samples later, I choose two wines, pay with plastic.

Abuelo presents me with three bottles. Confused,
I argue in labored Spanish with pleading eyes.
Apologetic, he produces a hundred quetzales in cash.

We shake hands and I leave satisfied with two bottles
of richly flavored Guatemalan artisan wine:
a mead and a raspberry-infused rose.

Un Poco Loco

Three thousand miles out of my element,
my nightly fight-or-flight response jolts me
from this dorm-style bed in San Pedro.

I trip the flashlight switch on my smart phone,
cautious not to startle my companion, when
something black, creepy, and quick scampers
across the ceramic floor.

Scorpion? I stifle my gasp, then appraise
The situation with a longer look.
Only a cockroach, I note, with little consolation.
I grab my shoe and with more gusto than needed,
smack it quick, then grind its shell and guts
until its final wriggle ceases.
Brushing the remains beneath the bed, I continue
to the kitchen for a one a.m. coffee.

All at once, a strange cat shrieks, fur on end, tearing
around a corner. Then a familiar chorus
from the triad of resident dogs. The chase is on.

Daena appears in the kitchen, shaking her head.
I recount the roach tale. She pounds her fist
on the table with barely a sound.

*That explains it! I dreamed I stomped a turtle,
killed it, then recognized it as your guardian animal.
Now, here you are, killing cockroaches in our dorm.*

I wonder, though, what it explains: a latent desire to murder me
or the reason three beers with chips and salsa picante
is not a wise choice for a bedtime snack.

Alone in the Andes

In Villa de Leyva, there's a pilgrimage
and it's required, almost, but
my heart, head, and muscles groan
as Sara strides while I drag
foot after hand after face,
panting, cursing thirty years of smoking,
forty pounds impeding weight.

Resting just until she reaches the corner
that takes her beyond sight,
I climb a few yards more until
Sara insists that the ridge I straddle,
a third up, is my safe point, and forced
into a choice made for me, questions
pinball inside my head, but I ask only,

How long?

because waiting is forever without a watch
and I beg a photo for proof, nod goodbye,
then sit alone, a garden of rooftops
unfolding before me, but inside,

empty landscapes where no one holds my hand
or knows my name, and fear,
fiercer than banditos, cougars, and flash floods
sets in until, quivering,

I face an even greater challenge,
seeking balance in the steepest place I know.

About the Author

Lynn Ciesielski had a fulfilling career working with children and adults with various disabilities. She taught for eighteen years in the public schools and worked another ten in the private sector. After taking an early retirement, she began to dedicate a lot of her time to reading, studying, and writing poetry and also hosted several poetry series around Western New York.

Her work has appeared in *Iodine Poetry Journal, Main Street Rag, Buffalo News,* and *Wild Goose Poetry Review,* among others. Her chapbook, *I Speak in Tongues,* was published by Foothills in 2012 and her full-length collection, *Two Legs Toward Liverpool,* was published by Main Street Rag in 2015. In addition, she has several works in each of two anthologies self-published by her critique group, LitGarden Writers. They are titled *Just Twelve More Poems and Other Works,* and *Tilting Toward the Moon,* and came out in 2019 and 2023, respectively.

www.ingramcontent.com/pod-product-compliance
Lightning Source LLC
Chambersburg PA
CBHW070941160426
43193CB00011B/1769